# The Unitarian Universalist
## Pocket Guide

D0375608

# The Unitarian Universalist Pocket Guide

Edited by Peter Morales

Fifth Edition

Skinner House Books
Boston

www.skinnerhouse.org

Printed in the United States

Cover and text design by Suzanne Morgan
Photos from UUA archive/Nancy Pierce. Photo on page 21 by Harry Carnes. Used by permission.

print ISBN: 978-1-55896-606-2
eBook ISBN: 978-1-55896-577-5

6 5 4 3 2 1
15 14 13 12

Library of Congress Cataloging-in-Publication Data
The Unitarian Universalist pocket guide.—5th ed. / edited by Peter Morales.
    p. cm.
  Includes bibliographical references.
  ISBN 978-1-55896-606-2 (pbk. : alk. paper)—ISBN 978-1-55896-577-5 (ebook)
 1. Unitarian Universalist Association. 2. Unitarian Universalist Association. I. Morales, Peter.
  BX9841.3.U55 2012
  289.1'32—dc23
                                                        2011041691

We gratefully acknowledge permission to reprint "Come, come, whoever you are" by Rumi, translated by Coleman Barks; and an excerpt from "The Rose of Hafiz" by Mark Belletini, copyright © 2008.

TO LEARN MORE about Unitarian Universalism or to locate a congregation near you, please write to the Unitarian Universalist Association, or visit the Unitarian Universalist Association website. We welcome you to join us as we strive to work and worship together with respect, openness, and understanding.

**Unitarian Universalist
Association of Congregations**
25 Beacon Street
Boston, MA 02108-2800
(617) 742–2100
www.uua.org

The largest Unitarian Universalist congregation is the Church of the Larger Fellowship, which provides a ministry for isolated individuals, small groups, and those unable to attend a Unitarian Universalist congregation in person. Members live all over the world and interact with the Boston-based church staff by mail, phone, and email.

**Church of the Larger Fellowship**
25 Beacon Street
Boston, MA 02108–2800
(617) 948–6166
www.clfuu.org

# Contents

# Unitarian Universalist Principles

We, the member congregations of the Unitarian Universalist Association, covenant to affirm and promote:

The inherent worth and dignity of every person;

Justice, equity, and compassion in human relations;

Acceptance of one another and encouragement to spiritual growth in our congregations;

A free and responsible search for truth and meaning;

The right of conscience and the use of the democratic process within our congregations and in society at large;

The goal of world community with peace, liberty, and justice for all;

Respect for the interdependent web of all existence of which we are a part.

# Sources of Our Faith

The living tradition we share draws from many sources:

Direct experience of that transcending mystery and wonder, affirmed in all cultures, which moves us to a renewal of the spirit and an openness to the forces which create and uphold life;

Words and deeds of prophetic women and men which challenge us to confront powers and structures of evil with justice, compassion, and the transforming power of love;

Wisdom from the world's religions which inspires us in our ethical and spiritual life;

Jewish and Christian teachings which call us to respond to God's love by loving our neighbors as ourselves;

Humanist teachings which counsel us to heed the guidance of reason and the results of science, and warn us against idolatries of the mind and spirit;

Spiritual teachings of earth-centered traditions which celebrate the sacred circle of life and instruct us to live in harmony with the rhythms of nature.

# Foreword

You hold in your hand a slim volume with a big goal. This is an introduction to the faith community in which I have spent my life. These are the words of the ordained and laypeople, the certain and the seeking, the lifers and the newcomers, the beloved and the broken hearted, the insiders and the reject- ed, all of whom have found a home in the extraordinary, yet intimate, communities of Unitarian Universalism. Do not expect a clearly marked road map. This book does not dic- tate dogma because Unitarian Universalism is not attached to particular beliefs; rather it is committed to specific work-- striking a balance between openness to differing viewpoints on one hand and fierce advocacy of shared ethical claims on the other. This pocket guide hints at our rich, complex, im- perfect, and collective struggles to balance these goals while building diverse and supportive communities.

Unitarian Universalists have no set creed, but we do af- firm seven shared Principles (see the beginning of this book). If you join in fellowship with Unitarian Universalism, you can hold any opinion you want about the existence of a god and what to call that god. You can change your opinion over time. You can follow your conscience, your readings, your thoughts, and your desires on issues like the existence of an afterlife, the idea of sin, the value of prayer, or the authority of religious texts. Among our congregations, you will find many different worship styles: raucous and religious, contemplative and nature-based, intellectual and secular. You can pray or not, sing in the choir or mumble the hymns, rush out after service or help brew the coffee, collect the canned goods or organize the field trip, pass out a petition or let the petition pass you by, dress casually for services or don your finest attire. Having set aside divisive doctrinal battles we seek a straightforward commitment to the fluid, open, collective work of seeking our truths together without assuming that we will all share the same truth.

Sound easy? It is not. But it is deeply rewarding. The seven Principles are simple to state but challenging to implement. Building a truly expansive intellectual, ethical, and cultural community is not for the faint of heart. In this way, the dogma of Unitarian Universalism is procedural rather than theological. We are committed to being together and to being together in ways that respect our Principles. Our worship and our work exist in finding practical and nurturing ways to govern ourselves and our congregations by living out our commitment to openness, democratic process, human equality, social justice, and personal exploration without harsh judgment.

This little pocket guide suggests some of the reasons we keep going even when the work is hard and the outcomes are uncertain. In other words, this is a book about our faith. Our faith as Unitarian Universalists is not a specific claim about a particular god. It is not found in a single book. It does not rely on claims of our inherent specialness as individuals or as a people. Our faith is messier. Our faith is a belief that we can embrace the common good through how we interact with one another by holding fast to our precepts of inclusion, participation, and nonjudgmental disagreement. Our faith is a practice of intellectual humility, reminding us of our own limitations. Our faith assures us that we are not alone and that we can be part of something greater than ourselves.

If you have never heard of Unitarian Universalism, these pages will teach you something about our history, our faith, our worship, our religious education, and our social justice efforts. If you are new to Unitarian Universalism, these pages will help you learn more about the larger tradition of which your local congregation is part. If you are a lifelong UU, like me, these pages will remind you of our deep roots, our fierce commitments, and our continuing efforts. There is a great deal of information in these pages, but you will not find definitive answers to all your questions. In fact, you may find this book raises more questions than it settles, but that, of course, is at the very heart of Unitarian Universalism.

The journey is the joy. The companions are the comfort. The work is the faith.

Melissa Harris-Perry
MSNBC Host
Professor of Political Science, Tulane University
Lifelong Unitarian Universalist

# Preface

Thank you for your interest in Unitarian Universalism. Ours is a religion with deep roots in the Christian tradition, going back to the Reformation and beyond, to early Christianity. Over the last two centuries our sources have broadened to include a spectrum ranging from Eastern religions to Western scientific humanism.

Many people find this confusing. The first question most of us ask about someone's religion is, "What do you believe?" I am convinced that to ask what religious people "believe" is the wrong question. Beliefs change. None of us believes as an adult what we believed as young children. We should ask far more important and fundamental religious questions, such as: What do we love? What do we hold sacred? What moves at the core of our being? What calls to us? How do we aspire to live? What shall we do with our lives?

Similarly, people typically misunderstand the concept of faith. We have been taught to think of faith as affirming a set of propositions, usually in the form of assenting to a creed and doctrines. Actually, if we look at the biblical origins of faith in the Hebrew scriptures, faith is a relationship. Faith is about *being faithful*—faithful to what is sacred. The great religious leaders—Jesus, the Buddha, Moses, Muhammad—never showed interest in what people *believe*.

I like to call Unitarian Universalism a religion that is *beyond belief.* We won't ask you to try to believe what you find unbelievable. We do challenge ourselves to be faithful to our highest aspirations and to our most deeply held convictions. We do affirm fundamental values—like the inherent worth and dignity of every person and compassion for one another that calls us to act to allay suffering and work for justice. We affirm our interconnectedness. We are relational creatures. We become fully human as part of a community. We are also part of a natural order that sustains us and for which we are responsible.

So while we won't ask you to believe what you do not believe, we will ask you to love what you love and to be faithful to what you love. We commit ourselves to walk together, to heal what is broken, to support each other in life's journey, to make a difference in our lives and in the world.

If you are not already a Unitarian Universalist, I urge you to consider joining us. In our movement you will find wonderful, idealistic, committed and loving people. It might transform your life.

This *Pocket Guide* includes essays by some of our most distinguished leaders and some of my wisest colleagues. Explore. Reflect. Get to know us better.

Blessings,
Peter Morales
President, Unitarian Universalist Association of Congregations

It's a blessing you were born.
It matters what you do with your life.
What you know about god is a piece of the truth.
You do not have to do it alone.

LAILA IBRAHIM

# Our Faith

Come, come, whoever you are.
Wanderer, worshipper, lover of leaving.
It doesn't matter.
Ours is not a caravan of despair.
Come, even if you have broken your vow
a thousand times
Come, yet again, come, come.

RUMI

Unitarian Universalists are especially fond of these words by the Sufi poet and mystic Rumi. His lyrical verse offers a small glimpse of our religious vision—a faith and a world large enough, inclusive enough, for everyone. The fact that we, with our Puritan roots, find meaning in the work of a Sufi poet speaks to our openness to—indeed, our expectation of—finding truth and wisdom in the words of people from cultures and traditions quite different from those we might have grown up in.

Unitarian Universalism is a non-creedal faith. Rather than a common theology, we are bound by our common history, our affirmation of each person's spiritual quest, and the promises we make to one another about the spiritual values we uphold. Whether you revere God, Goddess, nature, the human spirit, or something holy that you have no name for, you are welcome to join any Unitarian Universalist community and to worship, study, work, and be in relationship with people who are all on their own spiritual paths. If you find over time that your personal credo no longer feels adequate to what you see and experience in the world, your Unitarian Universalist community will companion you through those changes. Your doubts and questions will never jeopardize your belonging. In this faith, which I serve most joyfully, we welcome doubts and questions, and we uphold one another amid all the storms of life.

There have always been people of faith like us: We are the people who sought a religion marked by freedom and reason and acceptance, in addition to faith and hope and love. Our forebears are martyrs who died for religious freedom, ministers who preached that no one is damned to hell or outside the reach of divine love, thinkers who taught us that no spiritual tradition has a monopoly on wisdom, and activists who focused our attention on bettering this world rather than placing our hope in the afterlife. We stand in a grand and glorious stream of faith, always flowing toward freedom, justice, and love of the world.

We are called by our faith to respond to the world, its sorrows as well as its joys. We are often heartbroken about the state of this world, but never truly in despair. We who are privileged to be part of this liberal faith have inherited an extraordinary legacy. We have been given the gift of freedom to believe or to doubt; the gift of reason, to consider what we know of life and compare it to the timeless wisdom from other cultures. We have received powerful examples of courage in the service of humanity and of a love that encompasses all life. These are treasures—but they are not ours to keep. They enrich each one of us, but only if we give them away, again and again.

Because of these religious values, Unitarian Universalists have always sparked social change far out of proportion to our actual numbers. We have been instrumental in the abolition of slavery, women's suffrage, the civil rights movement, the gay rights movement, and the fight for economic and environmental justice, among other things. We do this work best when we remember what church is and what it is not. Most importantly, church is not a place to hide. It is not the place to get away from the world. It is not a place where we all get to pretend that the life we live and our particular situations are not terribly complex, often confusing, and sometimes depressing. Church is the place where we stand with one another, look the world in the eye, attempt to see it clearly, and gather strength to face what we see with courage and, yes, with joy.

Unitarian Universalism is especially important right now, because something sinister is brewing in our culture and our world again: a harsh and hateful fundamentalism in both religion and politics that makes a mockery of discourse and a joke of fellowship, from the banning of Muslim garb in France to the bullying and suicide of gay teenagers. Unitarian Universalism, with its deep roots in democracy and in community, provides a corrective saving grace. We give religious freedom voice and hands and feet; we put it in the service of others. We know that nothing takes the place of community and connection, nothing is a worthy substitute for our ties to the Holy and to one another, across all creedal barriers.

We believe in this saving message. We believe in building and sustaining communities of memory and hope, in providing way stations of resistance for a people and a world battered by the relentless assault of intolerance. If you share our vision, we welcome your voice, your hands and feet, your restless heart.

Come, yet again, come.

ROSEMARY BRAY McNATT

Our faith is not interested in saving your soul—
we're here to help you unfold the awesome soul
you already have.

ANDREA LERNER

# Three Stories

## *Coming Home*

I invented Unitarian Universalism. All by myself. I know numerous other people who have done this as well. I did it on buses, traveling up and down Livernois Avenue in Detroit. I was seventeen or so, a working-class Irish Catholic, living with my parents and attending a Jesuit college about ten miles away. The Jesuits would have been astonished, I suppose, to learn that this is what they had fashioned: a teenager trying to figure out what religion was and could be, and whether it was even possible to be both religious and honest much less an actual member of an actual church. I thought not. Each day that bus went within a half-mile or so of a Unitarian church, but I didn't know that and, if I had known, it wouldn't have meant a thing.

A decade later in another city, long after I had left "The Church," I stumbled on a passage in a book that described Unitarian Universalism. I was astonished: This thing I had invented actually existed—a richer version than mine, a version with a religious, intellectual, and cultural tradition I couldn't have imagined, but still, identifiably mine. And then there was the experience so many of us have had—of coming home. Of showing up in this church and finding comfort and challenge and people who insisted that I grow, of finding ideas that thrilled and scared me because they demanded so much, of finding a community of scrappy, smart, satisfying people who cared passionately about the church, about Unitarian Universalism, and about leaving the planet a better place, people who believe that they need one another for religious and social reasons, and for the work of making justice.

Unitarian Universalists come from so many places: parents who want their children to be religious but not limited by creeds; community activists who want a religious grounding for their work; people who left a traditional religion because they grew uncomfortable with its message; those with generations of Unitarian or Universalist forebears; gay, lesbian, bisexual, and/or transgender people who want a religious community where they will feel welcomed and where their partnerships will be blessed; biracial families; couples from different faiths who join because they want to be married by a clergyperson who will respect and honor their traditions and then decide to stay. Many paths are traveled on the way to Unitarian Universalism.

But what about the folks who don't even know this faith exists, who have some sense of what they wish existed but can't imagine that it does? The kids or young adults or retired men and women on a bus somewhere in some city, longing for something that could be right around the corner or down a street from where they are. What about those people? How does Unitarian Universalism reach them?

A few years ago I had an experience that made me passionate about inviting others into my own, chosen, faith tradition. My brother was dying, the sibling I had always been closest to. For months I spent as many weekends as I could traveling from Boston to Detroit. Those weeks were fraught with pain and grief, but also with unexpected moments of something like joy. John and I and the rest of the family cried and laughed together, and odd and amazing things happened, because in the midst of this tragedy, this watching of a marathon runner curled on his bed like a child, there was space only for honesty.

Odd and amazing things happened, but none more odd and amazing than this: Johnny experienced a deathbed conversion. My Roman Catholic brother became a Unitarian Universalist.

He gathered us, his wife, his grown sons, and me, and asked that a friend of mine, the Reverend Terasa Cooley, then minister of the First Unitarian Universalist Church in Detroit (yes, the very church I had passed decades earlier), be asked to minister to him for his last few weeks and days. The memorial service was held in that church, attended by hundreds of people who couldn't sing the hymns. I smiled, honored to have witnessed this final act of integrity, and pleased to know that he and I were more alike than we had guessed. I was also sad that his life—so rich in most ways—had not been as religiously satisfying as his death. And conscious that the one person who might have changed that was . . . me. I had talked about Unitarian Universalism of course—it is central to my life—but the one thing I hadn't done, hadn't even thought of doing, was urge him to join me there.

This is what I have learned: For each time I don't reach out to someone who might join this faith, for each time I hesitate to be hospitable, out of shyness or solipsism, I may be leaving someone's life poorer than it might be. If there's a teenager on a bus somewhere—and there is—I'd like to offer her the good news of Unitarian Universalism.

KATHLEEN MONTGOMERY


## Being Found

> Amazing Grace how sweet the sound that saved a wretch like me. I once was lost but now am found, blind but now I see.
>
> JOHN NEWTON

These self-deprecating words were written by an Englishman who participated in the Trans-Atlantic slave trade. On May 10, 1748, his boat came upon a major storm and John Newton, in fear, began to pray. As the story goes, the storm calmed as he prayed—a miracle of sorts. When the storm subsided, Newton realized his God helped him through this trial. Later, as he looked back on the event, he came to understand it as a transcendent moment, that his God was giving him a message. This Apostle Paul-like experience moved him deeply; his consciousness was pricked and he was changed forever. He eventually left the slave-trading business to become a preacher. If you've read or sung Newton's words, you feel the passion; you know the writer was moved by something significant. You know the author of the famous hymn "Amazing Grace" was reborn in 1748. I can relate to Newton, but in a slightly different way. I was reborn nearly a decade ago. A storm raged in my life too, caused by family members and friends telling me that my religious viewpoints were unorthodox, outlandish, and weird. They chastised me for leaving the Christian church I was reared in. I felt alone, angry, and scared. Then, one day, I started reading a book about various Protestant denominations in America. As I got near the end of the book, I read something that changed my life. In fact, it rocked my world! It was a summary of Unitarian Universalism, its values and principles. I realized that I was a Unitarian Universalist and had been for a long time. The words came to me like manna from heaven and I ate every one. Newton's lyrics arose in my mind: "Amazing grace how sweet the sound that saved a wretch like me."

Soon after that experience, I found a Unitarian Universalist church that was exactly what I expected—warm, friendly, and open. I was home. Here I wasn't weird. Here I was fully human, fully accepted, and fully loved. I found a place that gave credence to who I was at my core.

I hope as you read this, that you feel moved and welcomed, as I did when I discovered similar words years ago.

Perhaps you, like me, find it hard to believe that such a religion exists. It's hard to accept—we are so infused with the mores and culture of our upbringing. It's hard to break that connection to our family and culture, even when it stifles our spiritual growth. Most people don't question their social and religious customs. Most simply follow the conveyor belt of life.

We come into life, as John Locke put it, *tabula rasa*—a blank slate—and our families, environments, and experiences fill us with ideas about God, nature, and reality—some good, some bad. And then we live to test these notions. As a result of our experiences, our awareness changes. We find love. We experience loss. We win, we lose. In that process, we can shed our innocence. I call this our first *Great Awakening*, when we see that life is not easy, it is not the same for everyone, and that many things we were told are not accurate. From that day onward, we either stop thinking about them or rationalize the ambiguity. But many keep thinking, and seek better answers. If you are one of these, you are a "free-thinker," an experiential learner, and perhaps a Unitarian Universalist who recognizes that life is a constant cycle of rebirth. The words of Guillaume Apollinaire come to mind: "Come to the edge, he said. They said: We are afraid. Come to the edge, he said. They came. He pushed them and they flew!"

In a real sense, we all start out mentally and spiritually lost and can sing in agreement with John Newton, "I once was lost." But being "found" is something else. Being found means you have moved beyond adolescence—when you believe what you are told—and toward responsibly seeking your own religious truths by being honest about who you are, where you are, and what you value. It means that you do not believe in something just because someone told you so but because it is what *you* really trust in your heart. It means you are not religious because you are afraid but you are pious because it adds depth, balance, and meaning to your life. Being found means, in the words of the great Unitarian Walt Whitman, that "you shall listen to all sides and filter them from yourself." Being found is not a destination but a journey. Are you ready to be found? Are you ready to take the next step in your spiritual journey?

JOHN T. CRESTWELL JR.

## A Different Church

I was forthrightly evangelized into Unitarian Universalism. I was thirty-eight years old, living in Maine, driving a snow plow for a living and feeling very sorry for myself when a friend invited me to his church. He said it was different. I rudely refused. I cursed his church. "All blank-ing churches are the same," I informed him. "They say they're open—but they don't want queer folk. To heck with church!" My friend persisted. He *knew* his church was different. He told me his church cared about people, embraced diverse families, and worked to make a better world. He assured me I could come and not have to hide any aspects of myself. So I went.

And I dressed sooooo . . . *carefully* for my first Sunday visit. I spiked my short hair straight up into the air. I dug out my heaviest, oldest work boots, the ones with the chain saw cut that exposed the steel toe. I got my torn blue jeans and my leather jacket. There would be not a shred of ambiguity this Sunday morning. They would embrace me in my full Amazon glory, or they could fry ice. I carefully arranged my outfit so it would highlight the rock-hard chip I carried on my shoulder, I bundled up every shred of pain and hurt and betrayal I had harbored from every other religious experience in my life, and I lumbered into that tiny meetinghouse on the coast of Maine.

I expected the gray-haired ladies in the foyer to step back in fear. That would have been familiar. Instead, they stepped forward, offered me a bulletin, a newsletter, and invited me to stay for coffee. It was so . . . odd! They never even flinched!

They called me "dear." "Stay for coffee, dear."

I stayed for coffee. I stayed for Unitarian Universalism. Over time, the good folks of that church loved up the scattered parts of me and guided me from shattered to whole; from outcast to beloved among many. And those folks listened to me. I and my life partner became their poster-children for the brand new Welcoming Congregation program, designed to help congregations live into their values for effective welcoming of LGBTQ people. And they went on to provide important local pastoral and legislative ministries to gay folks in Down East Maine. We walked together and we helped each other grow.

Please don't think the transition was smooth or swift. These were not imaginary super heroes, they were human beings. And this was the mid-1980s. During the worship service on my second or third Sunday, a woman stood during Joys and Concerns to announce that all homosexuals had AIDS; all homosexuals were deviants who could not be trusted with children, public health, or civil society. All homosexuals should be quarantined, packed off to work camps to provide useful labor for society and keep their filthy lifestyle and deadly diseases to themselves.

As the member spoke I slowly sat upright from my customary slouch. I tucked in my arms, looked furtively around to see who might be glaring in my direction, and tried to remember if I had parked my truck facing in or out in the parking lot. In its journey of covenant, this congregation had just stumbled onto an important crossroad. But as Joys and Concerns continued, not one person made reference to the call to quarantine all homosexuals. The pulpit that morning was ably filled by a student from the local seminary. At the end of the sharing, the seminarian made a brief comment to assure us that not all the sentiments voiced this morning represented the whole congregation, and that was that!

Now I was at my own crossroad. I left quickly after the service. But what about next Sunday? Would I go back? Why on earth would I go back? That would be . . . well, you fill in the word—dangerous, stupid, foolhardy, looking for trouble, probably hurtful. But back I went. I was in the throes of learning my first lessons of being in covenant with a congregation. When we covenant to walk together through all that life brings, it means that when things get ugly, we don't walk away. Oh, how we may want to walk away! But our covenants call us to abide and work things through.

The next week, the regular minister was back. The service began as usual. I tensed up when Joys and Concerns came around. Someone announced something like a birthday, I can't fully remember. But I vividly remember that, one by one, folks stood up and awkwardly announced that not everything said last week was right, or true, or representative of who we were as a Unitarian Universalist congregation.

The crossroad had been engaged. The direction the congregation would take was being chosen. This congregation would not get stuck in conflict, mired in name-calling, or diverted from its gentle, steady trek toward building the Beloved Community. Our aspirations were unfolding, one voice at a time.

The congregation had passed a test. One among them had used language that depersonalized and endangered others. She tried to create a class of less-than-human persons toward whom violence would be acceptable. The congregation gently refused to follow. But an even more extraordinary and wonderful thing happened. The congregation also refused to depersonalize or dehumanize the original speaker. They did not start calling her names: "That homophobe!" "That gay-basher!" None of that happened. While the speaker tried to turn homosexuals into objects to be manipulated, the congregation never referred to her in a way that was less than embracing and respectful of her full humanity.

Later, in that same church, I opened the hymnal to find the words attributed to the Buddha, "Let us overcome violence by gentleness. Only through love can hatred come to an end. Never does hatred cease by hating in return."

My friend was right. His church was different. He forgot to tell me that, at his church, I could be in for a wild ride some Sundays. But he was still right. His church really cared about making things right for everybody.

GAIL R. GEISENHAINER

Instead of a creed, Unitarian Universalists share a spirit and vision of radical inclusivity, individual agency, and social justice. We create a safe space to stand out, stand up, and change your mind, particularly during life's transitions. We embrace personal discovery and growth through learning, engagement, and service. Our only doctrine is love.

VICTORIA MITCHELL

# Our Ministry

It is 1957. The congregation has gathered for the first annual blueberry pancake breakfast in my parents' back yard.
People are talking about buying a building, looking for a
minister, and mortgaging their houses to do it. Others are
recalling the service they put together on Sunday about
Hinduism, and how moving it was (or wasn't). One man,
in tears, pours out his heart to a couple of close church
friends, three old-timers pass around petitions, another
small group practices a song they'll be singing together a
week from Sunday—they have a ways to go. Two others are
actively debating the fine points of Transcendentalist spirituality. Worker-types pour orange juice, find more plastic
forks, and teach kids to flip the pancakes on the precarious
homemade grills. Children tear around the yard, the teens
are huddled near the pond, feeling obstinate about something, and blueberry bits are smushed all over the place.
When it begins to rain, the more muscular among us try to
push the first car (of a very long line) out of the mud.

More than fifty years later, I read in that congregation's newsletter that the annual pancake breakfast is coming around
again. Many would say that today's professional ministry is
about promoting long-term community, fostering spiritu-

ality, encouraging honest and intelligent discussion, raising "good" children, developing deep connections, working for social justice, creating music, sparking passionate group effort, and worshipping together. But I grew up in a small congregation that did not have an ordained minister, and I know that the members of a congregation can do all of this important ministry without a professional minister.

For Unitarian Universalists, the ministry we each practice with one another results in comfort, stimulation, fun, growth, commitment to the larger good, genuine help, and religious community. Each of us ministers to the others.

Yet we credential and ordain professional ministers, too.

## Beyond the Pancake Breakfast: What's a Professional Unitarian Universalist Minister For?

You may wonder just what Unitarian Universalist ministers have to offer. Imagine that you are in one of the following situations:

*I no longer believe in the God of my childhood. I want to know what the great thinkers say, I want to know what my options are, and I want somebody to reassure me that it is okay to follow my theological heart's desire!*

Chances are, your minister would enjoy this conversation! Credentialed Unitarian Universalist ministers have academic training and experience in a wide variety of areas, including, of course, theology. They may offer classes, spiritual groups, sermons, ongoing private discussion, and/or a reading list, if you are so inclined. Your minister will understand the spectrum of belief and unbelief and encourage you to find your own place.

Because Unitarian Universalists vary considerably in our individual views of spirituality, ministers are accustomed to supporting parishioners in a wide range of theological belief. Whether you are a theist, atheist, humanist, pagan, Deist, nature mystic (the list continues), you find yourself in a category known only to yourself, or you keep changing your mind, the minister will welcome you.

*My husband has just been pronounced dead. He's on the couch in the living room. I have no idea what to do.*

Your minister will come right over—ministers know about death. They can tell you what your options are; they understand the wide range of emotions you may be feeling and what needs to happen when. Your minister will be your companion during this difficult time.

Crises occur in life—your teenager didn't come home last night, the biopsy was positive, you lost your job, you need to find a nursing home for your father, you didn't mean to get pregnant or you desperately want to, you feel a crushing depression coming on, you feel aimless and empty, your partner is leaving you or you know you need to leave—these are all reasons to call a minister. Ministers are knowledgeable and supportive resources, and they have access to community referrals and congregational connections as well.

*I want to have a welcoming ceremony for my new baby.*

Our ministers frequently perform rites-of-passage ceremonies: baby dedications, weddings and commitment ceremonies, and funerals or memorial services. Talk with your minister about what the ceremony means to you and what you would like it to look like. Together you can design it.

*I like knowing that somebody cares about worship theory, congregational administration, social justice, pastoral care, ethics, church history, spirituality, world religions, committee dynamics, finance, religious education—you name it.*

During the course of their graduate work, our ministers receive training in all of these areas. During their ministerial preparation, in addition to traditional classes in theological school, they may meditate in a Buddhist monastery, teach a curriculum about Jesus to a sixth-grade class, work in a shelter for the homeless, study the Hebrew Bible with the Jesuits, organize fundraising events for a nonprofit agency, revive a moribund membership committee in a local congregation, design a website, manage a suicide hotline, or learn Greek. In addition, in preparation for professional ministry, our clergy must successfully complete internship and chaplaincy programs. Further, they try to live their lives religiously. They have committed themselves to the work of Unitarian Universalism, and they are there to serve you in the context of the religious community.

*I want to learn about the long-standing traditions of Unitarian Universalism.*

While newcomers to Unitarian Universalism are often impressed by the theological freedom in our congregations, they realize as time goes on that, in spite of the freedom, Unitarian Universalism is a "real" religion, with a distinctive history and culture. Although it is not a dogmatic religion, the newcomer will soon notice common attitudes and practices such as a respect for nature, a desire to seek justice, and a recognition of the worth and dignity of every person. Our ministers talk about, preach about, teach about, and live our particular ways as Unitarian Universalists. How do Unitarian Universalists relate to the world's problems? To whatever may be holy? To children? To those who do not feel empowered? How do we celebrate the holidays? Is this a Christian religion? Jewish? Pagan? Theist? Humanist? In what ways are we spiritual? Heretical? Academic? What are our hymns like? Where do we fit into history? Our ministers stand ready for conversation!

## Who Is the Minister?

In the Unitarian Universalist tradition, stereotypes about ministers don't apply:

Stereotype 1: *Ministers dictate what to believe.* In Unitarian Universalism, the minister helps all members of the congregation, including the children, develop spirituality, theology, and ways of being religious. Feel free to disagree with the minister! Talk it over!

Stereotype 2: *Ministers fit into a mold.* Unitarian Universalist ministers are people from a wide variety of racial and ethnic heritages. They are old and young and in-between, from every type of economic background. They are gay, straight, bisexual, and transgender, introverted and extroverted, sophisticated and down-to-earth, hilarious and serious. Our ministers will welcome you, whoever you are.

Stereotype 3: *Ministers judge people.* Our ministers are human, and they understand the human condition. Together, ministers and laypeople work to be the people they would most like to be.

Stereotype 4: *Ministers visit unannounced on Sunday afternoon.* When you want to see a Unitarian Universalist minister, say so! You can find a time and place that works for you—lunch at your office, at home with the baby, a scheduled appointment in the minister's study, at the nursing home, hospital, or prison.

Stereotype 5: *Ministers are the bosses of their congregations.* In Unitarian Universalist congregations, the members themselves, the laypeople, make democratic decisions. They ordain the minister, they "call" the minister to the congregation, and, if necessary, they can fire the minister. Members are ultimately responsible for the well-being of the congregation. The minister is not the boss of the congregation.

Ministers and parishioners collaborate to do the work of the congregation. We do our best to empower one another, whether we are designing a curriculum, planning a social justice event, providing support for a congregant in need, scheduling events that foster a sense of religious community, or developing the budget. While professional ministers lend their expertise, Unitarian Universalists honor the "ministries" that each of us offers.

Stereotype 6: *Ministers work for an hour on Sundays and are out of touch with the real world.* Most Unitarian Universalist ministers are engaged with the "real world" of people during the day, evenings, and weekends.

During the week, one might find a community minister running a board meeting for an after-school program, writing a press release about the community's response to a homophobic attack, conducting a senior citizens' chorus, or leading a silent retreat. Professional religious educators, in the course of a week, may counsel a child whose grandmother died, facilitate an adult discussion group about sexuality, adapt the preschool Sunday school curriculum, create a worship service, recruit volunteers for the youth group's field trip, and redesign the database for better Sunday school record keeping.

Parish ministers are equally eclectic. Of course they write sermons. But they also meet with the finance committee, the religious education committee, the youth group, the intern committee, the book group, the music committee—the list of meetings is long. They may review the budget, write for the newsletter, coordinate music for the Sunday service, answer email and texts, meet with parishioners, visit hospitals, help to develop long-range plans, and tend to hundreds of details. Meanwhile, parish ministers also work for social justice in the larger community.

In her poem "An Observation," May Sarton writes, "Move among the tender with an open hand," and "Stay sensitive up to the end." Ideally, that's what our ministers do.

When things are working well, our ministers love their calling. With all openness and sensitivity, they love the learning, they love the side of goodness, they love the inner spirit, they love the people. In the midst of checking their phones, driving like crazy from one appointment to another, coping with the dreaded sudden blank screen on Saturday night where the sermon text once was, just before someone calls to complain about what's gone awry at an overnight retreat for the youth group—in the midst of the dailiness of their jobs— they move among the tender with an open hand. They cry when their people are in pain, beam with happiness at human triumph, embrace the occasional moment of clarity on a Sunday morning, and have the privilege of working toward justice and mercy, with love.

This is our ministry.

JANE RANNEY RZEPKA

We Unitarian Universalists have inherited a magnificent theological legacy. In a sweeping answer to creeds that divide the human family, Unitarianism proclaims that we spring from one source; Universalism, that we share a common destiny. Unitarian Universalists are neither a chosen people nor a people whose choices are made for them by theological authorities—ancient or otherwise. We are a people who choose.

FORREST CHURCH

# Our Worship

"O thou beautiful . . . radiance. There is no day nor night, nor form nor color, and never, never a word." These luminous words from *Gitanjali* were written by Rabindranath Tagore, winner of the 1913 Nobel Prize in literature. Tagore wrote his evocative poems in Bengali and often translated them into English himself. I would like to think that Tagore's religious community, the Brahmo Samaj, which was influenced by nineteenth-century Unitarianism, nourished the spiritual depth of his poetry. The Nobel committee was so taken with the poetry's depth that one member urged his fellows to learn Bengali to better appreciate the original. I find Tagore's poetry, especially his *Gitanjali,* to be a compelling expression of the awe I see at the center of worship.

*Awe?* The sense of awe that hums in a mother holding her first-born for the first time. The sense of awe that shivers in a young man whose glimpse of the night sky suggests both his significance and his insignificance. The sense of awe echoing in an older woman who suddenly grasps the meaning of her own mortality. The sense of awe that affects true friends in the heat of an honest conversation. The sense of awe that kindles the heart of a man when he watches the morning sun strike his bedroom wall and realizes how glad he is to be alive in that moment, free of past or future.

"Awe" is the word I use to describe what seizes me when I realize that I live at all, that everything *is*, that hope is possible, that limits are to be expected, that tragedy is real, that control is largely an illusion, but that love is nonetheless desirable. "Worship," an ancient and very rich word, well describes my response to that awe: a sense of amazement, a sense of profound gratitude or acceptance, even a bodily trembling. Most often this kind of worship is both solitary and involuntary. I'd guess it is the most common sort of worship in the world, no matter the faith or doubt of the worshipper.

## Worship in Community

Worship has another, more limited meaning, however, that concerns us here. Worship may also describe non-solitary and quite voluntary experiences of artful celebration. The Holy Communion at St. John's Lutheran Church, Friday evening Shabbat service over at Temple Beth Shalom, Friday Prayers at Noor Islamic Center, Christmas Midnight Mass down at All Saints, and Morning Celebration at First Unitarian Universalist Church of Columbus are several of the names our spiritual traditions give this other kind of worship. Unitarian Universalists call this time the "service," "Morning Worship," the "Sunday Program," or just plain "worship." Though the content, style, or touchstones of Unitarian Universalist worship will differ from worship in a Friends' Meetinghouse, Greek Orthodox Church, Reconstructionist Synagogue, or

American Buddhist Church, all spiritual congregations share the idea of special times, particular ways to structure those times, and the central value of the gathered community. As with every other spiritual group, Unitarian Universalists range in our worship from plain to fancy, from "low church" to "high church," from singular to eclectic. There is no uniform style of worship, no agreed upon pattern of artful celebration among us.

The same is true of setting. Unitarian Universalists gather on Sunday in large rented homes, in striking modern buildings, in whitewashed New England meetinghouses, and in Gothic chapels splashed with the turquoise of stained glass. I know of one congregation that meets in a sort of outdoor amphitheater by the sea and another that meets in a converted barn. In these varied settings, you may find 600 parishioners gathered before a high pulpit or fifteen people sitting on simple wooden chairs in a neon-lit room.

In most of these settings the worship celebration usually lasts for about an hour. On rare evening occasions, such as the ordination of a new minister, the service may take longer. A midweek chapel, on the other hand, might last only thirty minutes. At a celebration like an ordination, you might see robes of rich color and elaborate rituals, such as the laying on of hands. At a regular Sunday celebration, you may see no gowns at all. Very often you will find that leaders of worship wear their finest daily clothes, and you will find the ritual to be relatively spare.

## The Order of Worship

Most Unitarian Universalist congregations have an Order of Service, a printed brochure that outlines the structure of celebration as practiced by that particular set of people. Musical preludes or chimes of some sort often begin our services of worship, calling us to attention and initial reflection. Opening words or invocations spoken by a minister or lay leader help us to remember how common worship is connected to our experiences of private awe. Sometimes a choir or the congregation will sing a verse of praise, often called a doxology. Longer hymns or songs of praise to the morning—or to Spirit, to Life, or to Love—are often sung close to the beginning of a service. Also at this point, a fire is often kindled in a wide-brimmed chalice. This symbol of our living tradition reminds us that we are neither the first nor the last persons who so gather. Other congregations light candles "of memory and of hope."

Our children often help to begin our worship celebrations. A story, a skit, a brief homily "to the child in all of us" will sometimes set the tone for the rest of the hour. Sometimes the whole morning is multigenerational.

In the middle of our worship celebrations fall a variety of devotional and community-building activities. Longer silences are sometimes introduced by a bell sound; prayers or meditations from the pulpit (or from the order of service) are sometimes read alone or with the group; image-rich guided meditations are sometimes included in the service. These

Dede Duson usher us into the wider world that we claim as our common home. We also have a Spanish-language hymn-book, *Las voces del camino.*

The words sung to these tunes are also revelatory. Originally, Unitarians and Universalists used Christian hymns with references to the Trinity and to hell-fire removed or recast. But for the last hundred years, writers have been experimenting with fresher language in order to move closer to the center of our historic tradition. For example, Unitarian Universalists refer to the Divine in ways often more poetic than doctrinal. "Spirit of Life," "Life of Ages," "Life of Life"—phrases such as these evoke a lively view of the Holy and help us to keep idolatry at bay.

## The Power of the Words

The Universalist insistence that salvation is for everyone, not just "the elect," now takes its practical form in the power of language to signify inclusion. Exclusively masculine language in hymns and songs tends to create a world where only men's beliefs, ways, and stories are valued, and fifty percent of the human race becomes invisible. To safeguard the belief in salvation for all people, Unitarians and Universalists have been making the shared language of hymns and songs broader, more reflective of the actual realities of the world. Thus, our hymns ought not be seen merely as artistic additions to the service but as true expressions of our religious sensibility. They do two amazing things. They express the reality that the earth isn't only populated by men, and they demand greater justice from all who sing of that reality.

There are other concerns, too. We live in a world where beige and brown people are rhetorically called "black" and "white," and where those called "white" claim a centrality denied to those called "black." Hymns that speak of every sin, every diabolical situation as "black" or "dark," and every grace or joy as "white" or "fair" or "of the light" seem to reflect the harmful rhetoric of a divided world. Unitarian Universalists who sing of the beauty of all colors not only receive traditions but also help to remold those traditions to help begin healing the world. It doesn't work like magic, but over time—and with humility of heart—it does work.

## The Sermon

A good sermon can provoke a decision that moves a person in a whole new direction. It can lift up a portion of our lives, holding it in just such a light as to reveal facets we couldn't easily see before. A good sermon can tug us further down the path toward a difficult forgiveness or remind us of our inestimable value as persons in a world that values little. Sermons can remind us of basic things we've forgotten, help us to learn and unlearn, show us how to reframe the seemingly impossible ideals so that we do not lose hope. I've heard sermons that have helped me question an easy faith, even wrestle with God.

Confessional preaching may invite us to be less tentative about our own truths. Prophetic preaching may rekindle a passion for justice on earth. Good preaching can bring us to the brink of awe no less than the evening star. A sermon may be read from a carefully crafted text or improvised after long mental preparation. It may be memorized or developed from notes. It may be long or short, prosaic or poetic. A sermon can be a dialogue between two people or a story acted out with dramatic props. In any case, the central part of most Unitarian Universalist worship is the sermon, the message, the homily, the talk.

## Readings

Readings are often shared before a sermon, but sometimes they are incorporated into the text of the sermon. These readings may be from just about anywhere. Spiritual readings, from both ancient scripture and more modern sources, are certainly commonplace. But the morning newspaper may feature just as frequently. I also use poems from various cultures and selections from novels or plays. But whether a story from the Gospel of Mark or a poem by Marge Piercy, readings help to root us. They remind us that we neither invented religious liberalism nor do we complete it.

## The Variety of Ritual

On certain Sundays you might experience rituals out of our taproot traditions, sacramental or symbolic events of soulful beauty. There may be a "breaking of bread," the ancient ritual of communion inclusively and freshly interpreted. A litany of *Kol Nidrei* may be sung during the Jewish High Holidays. Some of our congregations celebrate the Passover Seder in one form or another, Tenebrae on Good Friday, or the Eucharist on Maundy Thursday. The Flower Communion Festival, a moving ceremony that involves cut flowers, is a common Unitarian Universalist practice held on Easter Sunday or in June. These tangible symbols often prove more significant than either the sermon or the devotions, perhaps because they more effectively address us as whole persons, as bodies and not as mere minds.

Although sermons and rituals often come toward the end of a service, the actual closing of a service usually features a hymn and a blessing or a set of closing words. Often a powerful musical postlude will conclude the celebration.

Some of our congregations do not take up an offering, but the greater number do. The offering, whatever else it may symbolize, is certainly a summons to support an institution that nurtures and encourages liberal thought in religion.

In a Unitarian Universalist congregation, anyone can write a meditation, preach a sermon, or lead a worship celebration. Ordained ministers most often lead worship in our congregations, but lay members have also developed artful skills of celebration. Most of our congregations seem to have at least one lay-led Sunday per month, when an individual or group plans worship.

Some ministers work with a lay associate every Sunday. Guests may be invited: A congresswoman may speak on how her Unitarian Universalist principles guide her decisions, or an astronomer may offer observations on the stars that help elucidate the connection between science and religion. Lest it appear that ordained ministers stick to "spiritual" topics while lay members explore the more secular ideas, I should point out that Thomas Starr King, one of our great nineteenth-century ministers, used to preach brilliant sermons based on such natural phenomena as comets. He even managed to find lessons in the science of metallurgy!

## Rites of Passage

Unitarian Universalists join other religious folk in marking the great transitions in a human life—birth, coming-of-age, marriage or union, joining a congregation, covenanting with a new minister (ordination and installation), death and grieving —each may be celebrated with beauty, poignancy, and depth. It would be helpful to take a closer look at a few of these types of worship.

Marriages and commitment ceremonies most often occur on weekends at times other than Sunday morning. These are rarely more than a half-hour long and may take a variety of forms, but some public exchange of the couple's consent is usually part of the ceremony.

A memorial or funeral service may involve many people speaking brief remembrances, as well as familiar poems and psalms and direct words about death and grief. These celebrations of peoples' lives vary in length and tone, but I have never left one unmoved.

Unlike weddings or memorial services, the Sunday morning worship most often proves the best setting for the naming of a baby. "Dedication," "naming," or "christening" are the most frequently used terms for such a rite. Godparents may or may not be involved. One common form of such a service involves a rosebud and clear water touched to the child's forehead. Others use water alone, but there is no thought here of a child being born in sin and needing to be washed. "With water, which is as clear as your spirit, my child . . . " the minister may intone. Some ministers use the four elements —earth, air, fire, and water—as blessings on the child's body, intellect, passions, and spirit. The forms are varied, but the joy in such a ceremony is always of a piece.

In *Gitanjali*, Rabindranath Tagore wrote, "The same stream of life that runs through my veins night and day runs through the world and dances in rhythmic measures." Tagore also saw the waves of the sea and every flowering branch or blade of grass as part of that living "stream of life." The stately dance of the seasons, the lifeblood of the body, the breaking forth of the spirit—all of these tributaries flow into a mighty river that summarizes in its perpetual movement the power of worship in the living tradition. Tagore asked, "Is it beyond you to be glad with the gladness of this rhythm?" This question is nothing less than an invitation to leave the superficial behind and to embrace the life of the Spirit.

MARK BELLETINI

Unitarian Universalism is faith in people, hope for tomorrow's child, confidence in a continuity that spans all times. It looks not to a perfect heaven but toward a good earth. It is respectful of the past, but not limited to it. It is trust in growing and conspiracy with change. It is spiritual responsibility for a moral tomorrow.

EDWARD SCHEMPP

# Our Religious Education

In a Cherokee wisdom tale, an elder is teaching his grand-children about life. He says to them, "A terrible fight is going on inside me between two wolves.

"One wolf represents fear, anger, envy, greed, arrogance, self-pity, lies, false pride, and ego.

"The other wolf stands for joy, peace, love, hope, humility, generosity, truth, compassion, and faith.

"This same fight is going on inside you, and inside every other person, too."

The children were quiet for a minute and then one child asked earnestly, "Grandfather, which wolf will win?" The elder replied, "The one you feed."

A primary purpose of religion—and religious education—is just this: to nurture all that is right and good in us; to help us to be our best selves. And the lessons about the two wolves of human nature are best learned through stories. For people of all ages, individual and communal stories serve to ground us in our values, bond us together in community, teach us what we most need to know, and inspire us to bring more peace, justice, and love into the world.

Most religions have one core story. The narrative of Unitarian Universalism, like its theology, is diverse and dynamic.

Unitarian Universalists do not adhere to one creed or set of beliefs, but share moral values and guiding principles. Coming from many religious and cultural backgrounds, we bring an ever-growing anthology of stories. In our search for truth and meaning, we are free to draw wisdom from many sources, including the world's faith traditions, science, literature, nature, prophetic men and women, and our own lived experiences. It would be hard to identify anything that's *outside* the circle of wisdom possibilities.

### Teaching Faith, Not Creed

Theologian Paul Tillich writes, "There is hardly a word in the religious language—both theological and popular—which is subject to more misunderstandings, distortions, and questionable definitions than the word 'faith.'" This misunderstanding is particularly challenging for a liberal, free faith such as ours. Through centuries of religious history, *faith* has become synonymous with *creed*, *set of beliefs*, or *dogma*. Yet we have a different understanding. We believe faith is a journey we travel throughout our lives. A faith understood as a set of belief statements is fixed. But when faith means a journey, beliefs can change; values can deepen; understandings can broaden.

Grounded in the Unitarian story of freedom, reason and tolerance, and the Universalist story of faith, hope, and love, we teach that no one person, philosophy, or religion holds all the truth. We respect the diverse paths of religious experience and celebrate the diversity of humankind. We teach the inherent worth and dignity of all beings, so we work for justice, equity, and compassion in human relations. We teach that we are all moral agents, capable of making a difference in the world, challenging structures of social and political oppression, promoting the health and well-being of the earth. We take seriously the Golden Rule and the conviction to let our lives preach louder than our words. As UUA President Peter Morales says, "What we love is far more important than what we 'believe.'"

Unitarian Universalist religious education offers many paths to spiritual growth, addressing the need, in Gandhi's terms, for "the longing of the soul." In our programs, children and teens, as well as adults, might walk a labyrinth, explore the mysteries of nature, or engage in spiritual practices from yoga to gardening, from journaling to prayer. Each congregation decides how to structure its religious education experiences, but generally there are programs for children and youth on Sunday mornings, adult programs during the week, and opportunities for all ages to worship, serve, and learn together. Our approach to faith development is wholesome: it includes all aspects of being human—mind, body, and spirit.

## Touching Inward Springs

In 1837, William Ellery Channing, the founder of American Unitarianism, said, "The great end in religious instruction is not to stamp our minds upon the young, but to stir up their own; not to make them see with our eyes, but to look inquiringly and steadily with their own; not to give them a definite amount of knowledge, but to inspire a fervent love of the truth; not to form an outward regularity, but to touch inward springs." Unitarian Universalist religious education has deep roots in progressive modes of teaching that actively engage our heads, hearts, and hands in living our faith.

Unitarian Universalist religious education owes much to Sophia Lyon Fahs, a nationally respected religious educator and author, who saw religion as a natural human phenomenon rooted in one's own experience, not dependent on an outside authority. She saw the diversity of world religions as different cultural responses to universal religious questions, and believed wisdom could be found in all faiths. Fahs saw no conflict between science and religion, or between reason and faith. She developed curricula based on the Bible, world religions, science and nature, and multicultural studies and wisdom tales. The titles ranged from *Socrates: The Man Who Dared to Ask,* to *Jesus: The Carpenter's Son,* to *Water: Its Form and Motion.* "Life is religious whenever we make it so," she wrote, believing that we can find truth and meaning in all human experience.

A contemporary of Fahs, Universalist minister Angus H. MacLean, also left a lasting legacy with his insistence that "the method is the message." How we teach and engage in religious exploration is at least as important as the content we cover. You cannot teach democracy through autocratic methods; you cannot teach love without love, or respect without respect. "The effective method of teaching values," he wrote, "is itself the living exercise of such values." MacLean emphasized that religious education must respect the child's own experiences, and be highly experiential and personally relevant to prepare children to meet the social and moral challenges of their lives.

We are inspired, too, by progressive educators such as Brazilian activist Paulo Freire, who described education as "an exercise in freedom." Rejecting the "banking method" of education in which knowledge is deposited in the learner by the authority of the teacher, he showed that all are teachers, all are learners. "Humanization is the basic human vocation," Freire wrote, and he believed that through education that includes problem-solving and critical-thinking, people are empowered to change the world.

Our religious education model is based on a learning cycle that can be summarized with three questions: What? So what? Now what?

The *what?* is the initial experience. It could be a soul-stirring story or any new encounter such as a book, a film, a death, or a sunrise.

The *so what?* is where we find meaning in the experience, determine value, and gain insight. It's where we address the profound and universal religious questions:

~ Who am I? What am I called to do?
~ What is the meaning of life and death?
~ What is right and what is wrong?

~ What is the nature of the divine or transcendent?
~ Who is my neighbor? What is right relationship with them?

To these traditional questions, we add:

~ How much is enough? What constitutes ethical eating, consuming, and living in a world of unequal distribution of natural resources and financial wealth?
~ What is my responsibility to the earth and all living things?

*Now what?* asks, "Given what I now know, what I understand, and what I value, what am I called to *do*?" As Martin Luther King Jr. said, "Our lives begin to end the day we become silent about things that matter." In our religious education programs, children have made valentines and sent them to state legislators to support marriage equality. They have made dog biscuits for local animal shelters and adopted a rain forest. Teens have led interfaith service projects and supported literacy programs. Adults have fed the homeless and fought the root causes of homelessness. All have planted seeds; all are part of a new narrative.

## Multigenerational Community

We believe it is best not to write life's narrative alone. In *A Hidden Wholeness*, Quaker educator Parker Palmer recalls the time when farmers on the Great Plains, at the first sign of a blizzard, would run a rope from the back door of the house out to the barn. They all knew stories of people who had wandered off and frozen to death in their own backyards, having lost sight of home in a whiteout. Our faith communities can be ropes that help us navigate between one stage of life and another. Sometimes they are lifelines to guide us between just one day and the next. Lifespan religious education plays a crucial role in creating a safe, welcoming, and affirming religious home for people of all ages.

Busyness is the prevailing condition of our lives. Adults, adolescents, and even children find their lives highly scheduled, compartmentalized, and task-oriented. This busyness acts as a centrifugal force that pulls us away from family, friends, and other meaningful connections, and distracts us from our deep human need to reflect, renew, commit, and make meaning of our lives. In this compartmentalized life, the congregation is one of the last truly multigenerational gatherings, and Unitarian Universalist religious education provides opportunities for young and old to learn from one another. In our programs, for example, all ages explore the global threat to clean water, or wisdom stories from the Bible; teens and adults together plan and conduct service trips to the Gulf Coast; eighth-graders create an oral history of the congregation through recorded interviews with elders; and teens help children conduct an Audubon bird census.

For us, multigenerational community is not simply people of different ages inside the same building doing parallel play; it is people of different ages engaged with one another

—learning and teaching, working and worshipping, singing and serving together.

Rev. Susan M. Smith writes, "There is no such thing as a 'children's' story in a community of faith. The child, the youth, the newcomer, the elder all need a constant diet of shared imagery. Teach them forgiveness by teaching them 'Grudgeville.' Teach them abundance by teaching them 'Stone Soup.' Teach them the nobility of the human spirit by teaching about a little girl hiding in an attic who could say, 'In spite of everything, I still believe people are really good at heart.' Tell them the story of all ages. Tell them again and again."

### Diverse and Welcoming Community

Unitarian Universalism values cultural diversity, and religious education plays an important role in fostering multicultural congregations. Our programs affirm the diversity already among us, and invite people to bring all their identities and stories to enrich the tapestry of community. The curriculum *Building the World We Dream About,* for example, helps congregations authentically welcome and celebrate people from all racial and ethnic backgrounds. In programs for all ages, we reflect and affirm the rich cultural diversity that surrounds us and that our children increasingly know and live. We do not underestimate the challenge of building multicultural communities, but we try to approach this vision with open minds, open hearts, and significant amounts of humility.

*The Welcoming Congregation* is a popular program that prepares congregations—through education, inspiration, and action—to actively welcome, integrate, and support people who identify as bisexual, gay, lesbian, transgender, queer or questioning (BGLTQQ). Our nationally acclaimed comprehensive sexuality education series for children, youth, and adults, *Our Whole Lives,* promotes sexual health, responsibility, and justice for people of all identities. It has been a life-saving experience for countless youth who have found love and affirmation in this program when the rest of the world seemed hostile to their very being.

## A Story for All Ages

A woman dreamed she walked into a brand-new shop in the marketplace, one she had never seen before.

To her surprise, God was standing behind the counter.

"What do you sell here?" she asked.

"Everything your heart desires," said God.

Hardly daring to believe what she was hearing, the woman decided to ask for the best things a human being could wish for.

"I want peace of mind and love and happiness and wisdom and freedom from fear," she said.

Then, as an afterthought, she added, "Not just for me. For everyone on earth."

God smiled. "I think you've got me wrong, my dear. We don't sell fruits here. Only seeds."

The world needs a new narrative: one with more love, more peace, more joy, more justice. What seeds will we plant so that the world may harvest these fruits?

Religious scholar Wilfred Cantwell Smith says, "Faith at its best has taken the form of a quiet confidence and joy which enable one to feel at home in the universe." What a gift for our faith communities to offer: a home where people in all stages of life feel known and accepted as they truly are; a place to grow spiritually, live ethically, and find meaning and purpose in life.

JUDITH A. FREDIANI

Each week, there may be someone for whom our congregation is a lifeline. Maybe they need the tolerance and acceptance offered in liberal religion. Maybe they need a community to support and encourage their growing soul.... We hope to always be ready to welcome the stranger into our midst, and give them a place of shelter. As we gather together, we "let our light shine" out into the world, promoting peace, tolerance and justice.

BOB JANIS-DILLON

# Our Work for Social Justice

The rain is pouring buckets, but it doesn't stop the moving crowd of joyful people wearing T-shirts in sunshine yellow declaring "Standing on the Side of Love." The group of Unitarian Universalists is marching to City Hall to offer religious witness in support of marriage equality for same-sex couples. At the same time, in another city, Unitarian Universalist leaders from the "UU Ministry for the Earth" are being hand-cuffed and led to jail for an act of civil disobedience protesting drilling for oil and gas in at-risk wilderness areas. Meanwhile, in the mountains of Haiti, Unitarian Universalist ministerial students are talking and laughing with local Haitian villagers as they break bread together after a long day of laboring side by side to build an eco-village in the aftermath of the earthquake that devastated Haiti.

"Let us look more to our act than to our word to declare our true religion!" Rev. Dr. Peter Raible pronounced every Sunday at the close of worship for the forty years of his ministry. Throughout our history and in vibrant ways today, Unitarian Universalists are known for our work for social justice. In nineteenth-century America, Unitarians and Universalists were at the forefront of movements to secure women's rights, abolish the enslavement of people of African descent, and improve working conditions and wages. In the twentieth century, we answered Dr. Martin Luther King Jr.'s call to march for civil rights, to work for the alleviation of poverty, and to end the Viet Nam war. More recently, we can be found promoting ecological sustainability, countering fear and prejudice toward Muslims, advocating for undocumented immigrants, agitating for economic justice, and more.

Unitarian Universalism calls its adherents into the world, to engage with compassion and courage wherever suffering and injustice are found. As a spiritual path, this is a tall order, but we would not be who we are without social action as an expression of our faith. Ours is a religion of "deeds not creeds" and this emphasis is a direct result of the theological affirmations at the heart of our tradition.

Unitarian Universalists articulate these core affirmations in a variety of ways. We honor many voices, and celebrate many ways of naming and proclaiming our faith. But from our diverse chorus of voices, defining theological themes can be heard in ringing tones. They are voiced throughout our history, sung in our hymns, explored in our religious education curricula, preached from our pulpits, murmured in our prayers, and amplified in the writings of our theologians. They compel us to put our faith into action in the service of justice, equity, and compassion.

## We Affirm the Goodness of This World

Our faith begins with a radical yes to life in this world. We recognize life's struggles and acknowledge the painful legacies of injustice that haunt us and that dehumanize and fragment the human community. We seek to relieve the burdens of sorrow and exploitation that weigh heavily on people's lives; we work to waylay the fearful prospects of ecological collapse and the looming threats of nuclear war. But in the face of all that breaks our hearts and discourages us, we refuse a stance that regards this world as a fallen realm, a place of evil and corruption, or a wasteland bereft of beauty or goodness from which religion or spirituality offers escape. On the contrary, our activism springs from our deep sense of life's beauty, from our love and appreciation for this world.

At the beginning of the twentieth century, Universalist minister and theologian Clarence Skinner put it this way, even while World War I raged:

> We accept the world for the joyous place it was meant to be. We like it, despite the fact that belated theologians look upon it with inherited suspicion. It is no longer "the world, the flesh, and the devil," but "the world, the flesh, and God." The dominant motive is no longer to escape from earthly existence, but to make earthly existence as abundant and happy as it can be.

Skinner went on to urge people to be engaged in social reform, "Let us smash the injustices, tyrannies, the sins which imprison us and speed those readjustments which will make life here and now justify our hopes."

There are deep religious roots to this perspective. Unitarian Universalists embrace Biblical teachings as one of the sources of our faith. The Bible opens with the declaration that earth is a sacred creation, pronounced "Good!" from the beginning. Genesis tells the story of Jacob, sleeping in the wilderness with a stone for a pillow. He dreams that he sees a ladder connecting heaven and earth, with an endless circle of angels ascending and descending. When he wakes up he exclaims, "Surely this is none other than the house of the Eternal, and this is the doorway to heaven." The Torah pictures Moses calling his people to choose life that they might live in abundance and peace. The Psalms call people to "taste and see," to take wonder and delight in the creation. And though Adam and Eve are expelled from Paradise at the beginning of the Bible, later, in the Song of Songs, Paradise is found again in the joys of sexual love.

The Bible is full of earthy, practical ethics: bear one another's burdens, share your bread with the hungry, help the homeless, liberate the oppressed, visit the imprisoned, and love your neighbor as yourself. These admonitions are rooted in a spiritual affirmation of the goodness of life in this world. "Consider the lilies of the field," Jesus said to his disciples, asking them to observe the fleeting beauty of meadow flowers and the flight of sparrows to heighten their awareness that all life is provided for, and each person is of eternal worth. He went on to teach people to resist the oppressive ways of the Roman Empire, calling people to a life of non-violence and mutual care.

The down-to-earth beauty of this world compels our ethical response, a way of being that the great religious humanist

Albert Schweitzer summed up as "reverence for life." Many of the world's religious traditions inform our understanding of this insight. "Let the beauty we love become the good we do," the Muslim saint and poet Rumi cried. Native American spiritual traditions call for noticing the beauty before us, behind us, within us, and all around us. These traditions cultivate careful attention to the character of each living thing so that we can relate appropriately to the power of life and honor "all our relations." Some Buddhist meditation practices, similarly, foster a deep awareness of the "just-so-ness" of things, leading to an ethic of non-violence and care for all life. Unitarian Universalist minister and poet Mark Belletini reflects on our openness to the sacred revealed in the ordinary, and connects this awareness to the world's many religious traditions in "The Rose of Hafiz":

> The pebbles on which we walk
> are each one a new stone,
> a new *kaaba* fallen from heaven.
> That tree over there
> is the very one under which Buddha will sit today.
> And those plum blossoms? The prayer pennants
> fluttering above the monastery garden.

We understand that being attentive to the holiness right in front of us is a prerequisite for ethical living. If we fail to see life's goodness, we will fail to take action to protect it from harm—we will walk by suffering without seeing, and busy ourselves with unimportant tasks while glory surrounds us. Henry David Thoreau, one of our white Unitarian forbears who protested the enslavement of Africans in America, harkened back to Jacob's ladder to express this:

> I saw the fences half consumed, their ends lost in the middle of the prairie, and some worldly miser with a surveyor looking after his bounds, while heaven had taken place around him, and he did not see the angels going to and fro, but was looking for an old post-hole in the midst of paradise.

Thoreau, who advocated civil disobedience as a way to protest unjust laws, presages the spiritual perspective that runs through contemporary Unitarian Universalist commitments to social action: Devotion to life in this world opens the eyes and the heart to life's beauty. Thus awakened, we become fierce opponents of injustice as a contradiction to the good that is here, now, in this world—goodness that requires our advocacy, reverence, and committed love.

### We Affirm Salvation as a Possibility Here and Now

Because Unitarian Universalists affirm the goodness of this world, we locate the search for salvation as a this-worldly quest. We do not seek a heaven beyond this earth, liberation after death, or release from sin and guilt through brutal means such as the atoning death of a Christ on the cross. Rather, we believe salvation is manifest in the establishment of a common good in which people are free from oppression and want, and enjoy a fair and sustainable sharing of earth's resources. In our congregations, we encourage one another to seek joy in living simply that others may simply live, grateful for the gift of life. In this way we have a taste of paradise now.

Our Universalist forbears laid the theological foundation for social action that seeks the well-being of the whole human family. In contrast to those who preached that God would judge humanity after death, rewarding some with eternal life in heaven and others with eternal torment in hell, Universalist preachers proclaimed the all-inclusive love of God, whose grace would save all souls—leaving none behind. Rev. Gordon McKeeman makes the social justice implication of Universalism plain: "We are all going to end up together in heaven, so we might as well start learning how to get along with each other now."

"God's love embraces the whole human race," we sing in a contemporary hymn by Rev. Thomas Mikelson. To live from the perspective of universal love means breaking the patterns that divide people into the "saved" and the "damned." We seek to transform sexism, heterosexism, racism, and classism that privilege the well-being of some, while oppressing or exploiting others. For example, unjust economic systems and practices produce extreme gaps between the rich and the poor, enabling some to enjoy a super-abundance of life's goods while others die of hunger. Unitarian Universalists for a Just Economic Community work for "a world that sustains *all* living beings, where *all* people share the riches of the planet, where *all* voices are heard."

"Heaven" and "hell" are best understood not as humanity's destination after death, but as realities in this world. Hells of human-making are already here: injustice, abuse, genocide, human trafficking, torture and war crimes, destruction of eco-systems. Heaven can also be found in this world—in families and communities that embody love, in cultures that celebrate life and seek justice for all, in ways of living that relate to the earth with reverence and responsibility.

Jesus taught people to pray, "Thy kingdom come on earth as it is in heaven." Following the religion *of* Jesus, rather than the religion *about* Jesus, is a pathway to fulfilling this prayer. We seek to bring heaven home to today, and to transform the hells of human making. Grounded in love for life, our faith leads us to active work in this world to bless and care for life, and to repair harm. We labor in hope and in faith to promote equity, justice, and compassion throughout society: salvation, here and now.

### We Affirm the Interconnectedness of All Life

One of the principles of Unitarian Universalism affirms the "interdependent web of existence, of which we are all a part." This theological and spiritual declaration reflects the respect Unitarian Universalists have for science as a source of our religious convictions. Our faith concerns itself with the real and the concrete; we take seriously the actual world we live in and the discoveries science yields about it. Both post-Newtonian physics and environmental science reveal the interwoven and interactive nature of all existence. Even on the atomic level, the physical world does not consist of little bits of hard matter but is a relational dance of activity.

This religious sensibility is found in the writings of our theological forebears, such as William Ellery Channing, a founder of American Unitarianism in the nineteenth century:

> Through the whole range of nature we find nothing insulated, nothing standing alone. Union is the law of [God's] creation. Even matter is an emblem of universal sympathy, for all its particles tend towards one another, and its great masses are bound into one system of mutual attraction.

And as the Unitarian Universalist minister Kenneth Patton has written in *The Sense of Life*:

> We are all things, all persons, full and famished, good and bewildered, sly and honest, frightened and less frightened, killer and slain, the rapturer and the enraptured, youth and age, male and female. . . .
>
> We are all things, tree and flower, moss and grass, mammal and reptile, bird and insect. . . . Our fellowship reaches through the earth. We are river and stone, sand and mountain, fire and wind, comet and star.

Recognition of this interdependence and interactivity means that our ethical responsibility must take into account that our actions can have far-reaching effects. We cannot regard our life choices in isolation from their impact on ecosystems or on the lives of people half-way around the world.

This interdependent, global consciousness calls us to study the world, to recognize and analyze the large-scale systems in which we live—economic systems, patterns of consumption, political systems—with an eye toward answering the question: How shall we live so that we protect eco-systems, contribute to the common good, and help sustain rather than exploit others, whom we cannot see?

## We Affirm the Inherent Worth and Dignity of Every Person

Reverence and respect for human nature is at the core of Unitarian Universalist faith. We believe that all the dimensions of our being carry the potential to do good. We celebrate the gifts of being human: our intelligence and capacity for observation and reason, our senses and ability to appreciate beauty, our creativity, our feelings and emotions. We cherish our bodies as well as our souls. We can use our gifts to offer love, to work for justice, to heal injury, to create pleasure for ourselves and others.

"Just to be is a blessing. Just to live is holy," the great twentieth-century Rabbi Abraham Heschel wrote. Unitarian Universalists affirm the inherent worth and dignity of each person as a given of faith—an unshakeable conviction calling us to self-respect and respect for others. Historically, this affirmation can be traced to its deep roots in Jewish and Christian teachings. The Genesis creation story pictures humanity created in the image of God. Jews and Christians teach that human dignity is the gift given to each of us as our birthright;

we bear divine gifts and powers. It is our responsibility to recognize our sacred worth and realize our capacity to embody our likeness to God—our divine beauty, compassion, love, and creativity—in how we live and treat one another. The fourth-century Christian theologian, Macrina, expressed her regard for human dignity this way:

> The soul should know herself accurately and should behold the Original beauty reflected in the mirror and figure of her own beauty. For truly herein consists the real assimilation to the divine—making our own life to some degree a copy of the Supreme Being.

Our likeness to God can become tarnished or obscured, but it is never destroyed. The spark of the divine image remains within us all. William Ellery Channing extols humanity's inherent worth:

> I do and I must reverence human nature. Neither the sneers of a worldly skepticism, nor the groans of a gloomy theology, disturb my faith in its godlike powers and tendencies. . . . I know its history. I shut my eyes on none of its weaknesses and crimes. . . . But injured, trampled on, and scorned as our nature is, I still turn to it with intense sympathy and strong hope . . . I bless it for its kind affections, for its strong and tender love. I honor it for its struggles against oppression, for its growth and progress under the weight of so many chains and prejudices, for its achievements in science and art, and still more for its examples of

heroic and saintly virtue. These are marks of a divine origin
and the pledges of a celestial inheritance; and I thank God
that my own lot is bound up with that of the human race.

In the ancient Mediterranean world, the affirmation
that humanity bears the image of God was revolutionary. It
led women to claim their equal dignity and authority with
men and inspired slaves to claim their freedom from earthly
masters. Undergirded by these Jewish and Christian teachings,
oppressed people resisted the Roman Empire. They turned up-
side down the cult that deified the Emperor by claiming that
every person possessed the divine likeness. Scholars recognize
the seeds of democracy in this radical spiritual affirmation.

Unitarian Universalists stand within this revolutionary
stream of democracy and work to affirm human dignity
and rights. We passionately support the well-being and
thriving of every human being. We want every child, every
person, to have a full chance at life, to have their rights
respected, and their basic human needs supplied. Because
unjust social systems often oppress human thriving, and
curtail the full exercise of human gifts, we work to counter
economic injustice, racism, sexism, heterosexism, ageism,
ableism, and more.

Putting our faith into action takes organization. The Unitarian Universalist Service Committee, one of our leading
social justice institutions, "advances human rights and social
justice around the world, partnering with those who confront unjust power structures and mobilizing to challenge

oppressive policies." Through Unitarian Universalist Legislative Ministries established in many states, we work through the political process to advocate for issues such as marriage equality for same-sex couples, health care for all, and immigrant rights and protections. Our "Standing on the Side of Love" campaign supports UUs and other progressive people of faith to "rally local communities on behalf of marginalized communities."

## We Affirm the Power of Covenant and of Community

"What holds the world together . . . is trustworthiness, eros, love," writes James Luther Adams, Unitarian Universalist social ethicist. Our social justice work, ultimately, requires us to root ourselves deeply in love—to grow in love and wholeness ourselves—which we do through spiritual practice and our participation in religious community.

It is not enough to try to change the world. We know we also need to change ourselves. The poisons of oppression are often within us, as well as around us. We recognize too that our powers can be used for evil. We are capable of betraying one another, of acting with cruelty or shortsightedness. We can look out for our own good, while ignoring or exploiting others. We are submerged in social systems that collectively cause harm.

Building the beloved community that Martin Luther King Jr. called for requires personal spiritual discipline, self-examination, and transformation. Unitarian Universalists recognize that we must heal from internalized oppression, from unexamined prejudices, and unaccountable privileges. We must grow in the strength of our love. We must develop our capacities for moral discernment and choice, honing our wisdom and our devotion to use our gifts and powers in life-giving, responsible ways.

Religious community is imperative for us. In community we hold ourselves accountable to what we are doing with our powers, we practice prayerful discernment of what supports and protects life, and we share together in worship and spiritual practice, connecting us to the deep sources that empower our activism. In our congregations, as well as our seminaries, we create spaces for the deep work of facing oppressions within and around us, as we build our capacity to act for wholeness and liberation for all, including ourselves. Our "Building the World We Dream About" program, for example, "seeks to interrupt the workings of racism and transform how people from different racial/ethnic groups relate to one another."

James Luther Adams advocated for what can be called a "covenant of all beings." Covenant making and covenant renewing are among our core spiritual practices. In covenant, we bind ourselves willingly to one another, to all life, and to what Adams named "the creative, sustaining, commanding, judging, transforming powers, which may be interpreted theistically or nontheistically." These are the powers of relationship, interactivity, and creativity that support and uphold all life. Covenantal living engages us in living with and for one another and all of life. We are "brought out of our separateness into covenant" and take on responsibility for "the character of society and the love and preservation of nature." Adams writes,

The covenant responsibility is especially directed toward the deprived, whether these be people suffering from neglect and injustice or those who are caught in the system that suppresses them—that suppresses their own self-determination. . . . The covenant depends on faithfulness, and faithfulness is nerved by loyalty, by love.

Love is our source and our destination—our call and our response. We labor to keep faith with the generations of Unitarians and Universalists before us who stood up to dehumanizing systems and worked for justice, equity, compassion, and peace. We are inspired and challenged by their record of activism: to abolish slavery, provide redress for displaced Native Americans, reform prisons, establish free public education for all children, resist war, secure women's rights, abolish child labor, and protect workers. We celebrate that Unitarian Universalists have worked to end racial segregation and promote civil rights, legalize abortion, and promote equal pay for equal work. Today we work to put our faith into action, to carry forward this legacy of "deeds not creeds" as we labor to protect LGBT people and secure marriage equality for same-sex couples, support immigrant rights, work for peace and human rights around the world, promote economic justice, and care for the Earth. We do it all for love.

REBECCA ANN PARKER

Love is the spirit of this church,
and service its law.
This is our great covenant:
To dwell together in peace,
To seek the truth in love,
And to help one another.

JAMES VILA BLAKE

# Our Roots

Unitarian Universalists possess a rich heritage and many different ways of relating to it. Some argue that because we lack a shared theology, it is our common history that holds us together. Others relish the freedom to draw on multiple spiritual sources without being bound to any single tradition. Some take pride in knowing that unitarian and universalist ideas (notice the small "u"s) are as old as Christianity itself. Our "free and responsible search for truth and meaning" is more ancient still. Others stress the distinctly American flavor of our movement, noting that Unitarianism and Universalism (capital "U"s!) were born in the epoch of the Revolution. Still others tell the stories of our partner churches in Transylvania, the British Isles, the Khasi Hills of India, and the Philippines, insisting that their histories are our heritage as well.

## Ancient Roots

Given this diversity, one might begin telling the Unitarian Universalist story at many different points in time. UU Buddhists and UU Pagans claim a heritage that is older than Christianity. But most Unitarian Universalists trace their roots to the biblical traditions of Judaism and Christianity.

The ideas of "unitarianism," that God is one being, and "universalism," that God will save all humanity, can be found in the scriptures of ancient Judaism. For millennia, Jews have declared daily that "the Lord is one," and cherished the hope that "all the families of the earth shall be blessed."

These beliefs were part of the rich diversity of early Christianity. Searching the scriptures, some theologians found hope that all humans and even the devil would be restored to harmony with the divine. The official church refused to teach that this was certainly so. Yet Catholic and Eastern Orthodox theologians continue to teach it as a possibility. The idea of unitarianism was much more controversial. As the Roman Empire was becoming Christian, church leaders declared that Jesus Christ, the Holy Spirit, and God the Father were a Trinity, sharing a single divine substance. Those who found this unbiblical or too paradoxical created a rival church, with its own hierarchy and dogmas. Even after that church died out, unitarianism was despised as a heresy by most Christians.

Unitarianism experienced renewal at the time of the Protestant Reformation, in the sixteenth century. Protestants cherished the principle of *sola scriptura.* They relied entirely on the text of the Bible. Those who took this principle furthest rejected the idea of a state church, insisting that Christians should choose voluntarily to follow Christ's path. Among their modern descendents are the Amish and Mennonites. One small wing of this movement also rejected the idea of a Trinity as unbiblical. They planted churches first in

Poland and then Transylvania, where a Unitarian king embraced a policy of religious freedom.

The Polish church eventually disappeared, while Transylvanian Unitarianism survives today. Unitarian ideas reappeared in seventeenth- and eighteenth-century England and Ireland. Those who held them, including the philosopher John Locke, blended a commitment to biblical authority with the Enlightenment's stress on reason. Unlike the deists on one side and orthodox Christians on the other, they refused to choose between reason and revelation. Their first congregation was the Essex Street Chapel. Organized in 1774 by a former Anglican priest named Theophilus Lindsey, it set the tone for similar congregations in the American colonies. Universalist ideas were also promoted in England during these years, first by the mystical Philadelphia Society led by Jane Leade in the late seventeenth century. A century later, revivalist James Relly taught universalism on the grounds that Christ had died to save not individuals but all humanity as a single body.

## American Founding

Though European movements influenced their North American sisters, the origin of Universalism and Unitarianism in the United States did not involve the transplanting of European institutions to new soil. Nor was there a single "founding moment" for either tradition. Several different groups held unitarian or universalist beliefs. They came together only gradually.

The first people in North America to teach universal salvation may have been Germans who came to Pennsylvania for religious freedom. Their mystical Christianity also inspired them to live in celibate community, practice alchemy, and wait for the end of the world. The first explicitly Universalist congregation was planted in Gloucester, Massachusetts, by John Murray, an English immigrant who had learned from James Relly that an all-powerful God had predestined everyone to be saved. But the largest number of early Universalists came out of Baptist churches in western New England. Skeptical of educated ministers, they read the Bible for themselves and cherished debates with neighbors who read it differently. These diverse communities began to organize a General Convention in 1790. They had little in common other than their belief in universal salvation and a fierce opposition to state-sponsored religion. This put them in conflict with the Puritan or "Standing Order" congregations of New England, which received tax support well into the nineteenth century.

The first Unitarian congregations in the United States were inspired by Englishman Joseph Priestley. Priestley was a chemist who discovered oxygen, a friend of Thomas Jefferson, and a theologian who insisted that Jesus was no more than human. In 1784, his writings convinced the minister of King's Chapel in Boston to eliminate references to the Trinity from that congregation's liturgy. Ten years later, Priestley immigrated to the United States and helped found congregations in Philadelphia and rural Pennsylvania.

Like the Universalists, Priestley was wary of state-sponsored religion. But ironically, several Standing Order churches in the neighborhood of Boston embraced a milder form of Unitarianism. They believed that Jesus was more than human but less than divine. They also stressed the goodness of humanity. While their Puritan ancestors had seen humans as depraved, they had absorbed the optimistic Enlightenment philosophy taught at Harvard College. The debate over these new ideas caused a schism among the churches in Massachusetts. Though the Unitarians were reluctant to separate from their more orthodox brothers and sisters, they created the American Unitarian Association in 1825.

Each fledgling denomination had a theological champion. The Universalists' Hosea Ballou was a fiery debater who delighted in clever interpretations of the Bible. He taught that Jesus had died not to appease an angry God but to soften the hard hearts of humanity. And he took the radical position that even the worst sinners will go straight to heaven. Other Universalists speculated that some would be purified by temporary hellfire.

The Unitarians' William Ellery Channing was a reluctant radical. He loved peace, and helped organize opposition to the War of 1812. He hesitated to organize a separate denomination, but eventually became its most eloquent spokesman. He also hesitated to speak out against slavery. When abolitionist friends persuaded him to join their cause, he found himself alienated from the wealthy congregation he had served for decades.

Though Channing was a Unitarian and Ballou a Universalist, each man appreciated aspects of the other tradition. Ballou was a proud champion of Priestleyan unitarianism. Channing was not a universalist, but his faith in the human capacity to grow in likeness to the divine drew on the same spiritual streams as ancient universalism. The two men scarcely acknowledged one another, though they ministered in the same Boston neighborhood. Today's Arlington Street Church is heir to both of their congregations.

Ministers were not the only people who helped build up the two traditions. John Murray's wife, Judith Sargent Murray, was a powerful leader and advocate of women's rights. She began demanding equal access to education in 1779, and composed the first Universalist catechism three years later. Lucy Barns was disabled by asthma, but wrote letters to spread the Universalist faith. Catharine Sedgwick, one of the nation's most popular writers, incorporated Unitarian themes into her novels. Unitarian Hannah Adams expressed her liberal religious convictions in one of the first dictionaries of world religions.

## Heretics, Reformers and Institution Builders

Three different sorts of leaders helped nineteenth-century Unitarianism and Universalism evolve. First, there were the heretics—unfettered thinkers who reached beyond inherited theologies. Abner Kneeland, who called himself a pantheist rather than a Christian, left the Universalist ministry to lead Boston's Society of Free Enquirers. He was the last person jailed for blasphemy in the United States. Ralph Waldo Emerson shocked the faculty of Harvard Divinity School by urging future ministers to preach from their own souls rather than from scripture. The Transcendentalist movement he launched transformed American literature as well as the Unitarian ministry. During the 1850s, roughly half of all Universalist ministers embraced the Spiritualist movement, which sought a scientifically verifiable path to religious truth. A generation later, Unitarians and Universalists were the first to embrace Darwinian science as an ally rather than an enemy of faith.

Other Unitarians and Universalists were reformers. The heart of their religion was building a more just and inclusive society. Universalist shoemaker William Heighton helped launch the labor movement by calling for a political party composed entirely of "Working Men." The brothers Charles and John Murray Spear, both Universalist ministers, befriended prisoners and fought to end the death penalty. Unitarian Lydia Maria Child risked her career as a writer of children's books by demanding immediate abolition of slavery. Ministers Theodore Parker and Thomas Wentworth Higginson were so opposed to slavery that they took up arms to defend fugitives from the South. Adin Ballou, who served both Unitarian and Universalist congregations, was a staunch abolitionist, absolute pacifist, and creator of a utopian community. His writings on nonviolence inspired Leo Tolstoy and Mohandas Gandhi. Universalist and Unitarian women were among the first to be ordained in the United States. Antoinette Brown Blackwell and Olympia Brown combined ministry with agitation for women's suffrage.

Contemporary Unitarian Universalists cherish the memory of the heretics and the reformers. But we would not remember them at all if it weren't for the institution builders. Among the Unitarians, denominational president Henry Whitney Bellows led the way in making space for both Transcendentalists and liberal Christians in a single church. And the Universalists' "grasshopper missionary," Quillen Shinn, hopped to many unlikely corners of America with the message of God's limitless love.

## Reaching Out

Unitarians and Universalists never held a monopoly on liberal religion. Many Unitarian Universalists today hold views similar to the eighteenth-century deists and nineteenth-century Freethinkers. Those groups taught a "religion of reason" that only gradually found a home in our tradition. Some of the founders of Unitarianism and Universalism were active Freemasons, and from that tradition they took a commitment to religious tolerance and brotherly love. Unitarians and Universalists have long felt a kinship with the Quaker tradition, with its emphasis on the "inner light" in each person. They also reached out to the Reform movement in Judaism, which stressed ethics over ritual. The Ethical Culture movement founded by a rabbi's son, Felix Adler, abandoned belief in God altogether and worked closely with the radical wing of Unitarianism.

By the turn of the twentieth century, many Congregationalists, Methodists, and other Protestants were preaching a liberal theology similar to that of the Unitarian and Univer-salist founders. They also proclaimed a "social gospel": true religion was about building a better world. Unitarians and Universalists worked closely with them. At Harvard, Fran-cis Greenwood Peabody introduced sociology into the cur-riculum for future ministers. More radical activists created organizations that we now think of as secular. Universalist Charles Vail was the national organizer of the Socialist Party. Unitarian Roger Baldwin was the first leader of the American Civil Liberties Union. Unitarians Mary White Ovington and John Haynes Holmes were among the founders of the Na-tional Association for the Advancement of Colored People. With Universalist Clarence Skinner, Holmes also launched a network of activist "community churches." Among them was Egbert Ethelred Brown's Harlem Community Church, an important meeting place for African Americans and West Indians, and for black socialists and nationalists. Reformers like Holmes, Brown, and Skinner worked closely with a new wave of heretics. Calling themselves "humanists," these here-tics put their faith in science and humanity rather than God. Humanist leaders John Dietrich and Curtis Reese both came to Unitarianism from more conservative denominations. Several Unitarians and one Universalist, Clinton Lee Scott, signed the "Humanist Manifesto" that announced their ideas to the world. Meanwhile, other Universalists redefined their tradition to focus on the wisdom of all world faiths.

Once again, institution builders were flexible enough to win the heretics back. As leader of the Massachusetts Universalists, Scott invited a Unitarian humanist named Kenneth Patton to launch an experimental congregation. Its members studied global faiths and contemporary science, treating their church as a workshop for the future. Unitarian president Frederick May Eliot embraced humanists and reached out to Universalists, hoping both groups would help him build a united liberal church.

Unitarianism finally transcended its New England roots through the fellowship movement of the 1940s, 1950s, and 1960s. In communities from Montgomery, Alabama, to Boulder, Colorado, lay people created congregations without ministerial oversight. Many were closely tied to colleges or research centers. Others provided a religious home for radical activists in conservative neighborhoods. Some of the fellowships have grown into thousand-member congregations. Others remain small and feisty.

## Toward Beloved Community

The new congregations brought their energy into the Unitarian Universalist Association, founded in 1961 as the fruit of Eliot's dream. Many congregations and individuals still proudly call themselves "Unitarian" or "Universalists." Others, especially those who have come to the tradition since consolidation, claim a fully "Unitarian Universalist" identity. Unitarian Universalists played a vital role in the social change movements of the 1960s. Building on the legacy of the NAACP founders, Unitarian minister Homer Jack helped launch the northern sit-in movement in the 1940s, and he guided our tradition's social justice work in the 1960s. Most of the white lawyers who supported Martin Luther King Jr.'s work in Montgomery were members of the local UU fellowship. Unitarian Universalist minister James Reeb and Unitarian Universalist housewife Viola Liuzzo were martyred in Selma, Alabama, where they had joined hundreds of UU ministers in response to the murder of a local African-American activist named Jimmie Lee Jackson. Reeb had been a community minister at Boston's Arlington Street Church. Two years later, that same congregation hosted an interfaith liturgy at which opponents of the Viet Nam War prayed together as they burned their draft cards.

Not everyone agreed on the best way to foster justice and peace. Many Unitarian Universalists, both white and black, embraced the Black Power movement of the late 1960s. They hoped that economic and cultural empowerment would make beloved community possible. Others feared that Black Power was a betrayal of the integrationist ideal. The General Assembly of 1968 committed $1 million to black-led economic development projects. Debate over that decision consumed the denomination for the next two years. Leaders reduced funding for empowerment, citing a budget crisis. People on both sides left the tradition, hurt and angry. Others stayed or returned, making the struggle against racism and for beloved community one of our defining commitments.

Unitarian Universalism responded more comfortably to feminism and LGBT liberation. When Rev. James Stoll came out as gay in 1969—the first minister in any tradition to do so—he was embraced by other Unitarian Universalists. Our pioneering sexuality education curriculum, *About Your Sexuality*, was expanded to honor sexual diversity. Similarly, a small contingent of women ministers swelled to a majority within a few decades. The 1977 Women and Religion resolution began a process of removing sexist language and practices from our shared life. As women explored goddess-centered practices, they made neo-paganism an integral part of the spiritual mosaic of our faith.

If the late 1960s were the tumultuous adolescence of Unitarian Universalism, our movement has since settled into a stable maturity. Membership declined in the 1970s but has grown since then. This is because of our appeal to spiritual seekers, social activists, and interfaith families. In most UU congregations today, Christians, humanists, Jews, Buddhists, pagans, seekers, and others build religious community together. We join in the fight for immigrant rights and for marriage equality, and we help one another find sustaining spiritual practices. Our diverse national leadership guides us on the journey toward beloved community. As we continue moving forward, we look back with gratitude to the heretics, reformers, and institution builders who came before us.

DAN McKANAN

# Resources

*UU World*, the magazine of the Unitarian Universalist Association of Congregations (UUA), aims to help its readers build their faith and act on it more effectively in their personal lives, their congregations, their communities, and the world. The print magazine is published quarterly in February, May, August, and November. You can subscribe or read a weekly issue of the free online edition at www.uuworld.org.

The UUA also publishes a number of pamphlets intended to answer questions you may have about Unitarian Universalism. You can read these online by visiting www.uua.org/pamphlets.

*The following books are available from the UUA Bookstore: 25 Beacon Street, Boston, MA 02108–2800, telephone (800) 215-9076, website www.uua.org/bookstore.*

George Kimmich Beach. *Questions for the Religious Journey: Finding Your Own Path.* Boston: Skinner House Books, 2002.

Ellen Brandenburg, ed. *The Seven Principles in Word and Worship.* Boston: Skinner House Books, 2007.

John A. Buehrens. *Universalists and Unitarians in America: A People's History.* Boston: Skinner House Books, 2011.

John A. Buehrens and Forrest Church. *A Chosen Faith: An Introduction to Unitarian Universalism,* 2nd ed. Boston: Beacon Press, 1998.

Kenneth W. Collier. *Our Seven Principles in Story and Verse: A Collection for Children and Adults.* Boston: Skinner House Books, 1997.

Dorothy May Emerson, ed. *Standing Before Us: Unitarian Universalist Women and Social Reform, 1776–1936.* Boston: Skinner House Books, 1999.

Patricia Frevert, ed. *Welcome: A Unitarian Universalist Primer.* Boston: Skinner House Books, 2009.

Edward A. Frost, ed. *With Purpose and Principle: Essays about the Seven Principles of Unitarian Universalism.* Boston: Skinner House Books, 1998.

Susan A. Gore and Keith Kron, eds. *Coming Out in Faith: Voices of LGBTQ Unitarian Universalists.* Boston: Skinner House Books, 2011.

Mark Harris. *The A to Z of Unitarian Universalism.* Lanham, Md.: Scarecrow Press, 2009.

Jack Mendelsohn. *Being Liberal in an Illiberal Age: Why I Am a Unitarian Universalist.* Boston: Skinner House Books, 1995.

Tom Owen-Towle. *Freethinking Mystics with Hands: Exploring the Heart of Unitarian Universalism.* Boston: Skinner House Books, 1998.

Paul Rasor. *Faith Without Certainty: Liberal Theology in the 21ˢᵗ Century.* Boston: Skinner House Books, 2008.

Warren R. Ross. *The Premise and the Promise: The Story of the Unitarian Universalist Association.* Boston: Skinner House Books, 2001.

Jane Ranney Rzepka. *From Zip Lines to Hosaphones: Dispatches from the Search for Truth and Meaning.* Boston: Skinner House Books, 2011.

Frank Schulman. *This Day in Unitarian Universalist History: A Treasury of Anniversaries and Milestones from 600 Years of Religious Tradition.* Boston: Skinner House Books, 2004.

**For Children**

Pamela Baxter. *A Cup of Light: All About the Flaming Chalice.* Illustrated by Terry Stafford. Boston: Skinner House Books, 2011.

Jennifer Dant. *Everybody Is Important: A Kids' Guide to Our Seven Principles.* Boston: Skinner House Books, 2011.

Jennifer Dant. *Unitarian Universalism Is a Really Long Name.* Boston: Skinner House Books, 2006.

Patricia Frevert, ed. *Sunday and Every Day: My Little Book of Unitarian Universalism.* Boston: Skinner House Books, 2010.